SCIENCE FILES
PLASTICS

SCIENCE FILES – PLASTICS
was produced by

David West 👫 Children's Books

7 Princeton Court
55 Felsham Road
London SW15 1AZ

Designers: Rob Shone, Fiona Thorne, David West
Editor: James Pickering
Picture Research: Carrie Haines

First published in Great Britain in 2001 by
Heinemann Library, Halley Court, Jordan Hill,
Oxford OX2 8EJ, a division of Reed Educational and
Professional Publishing Limited.

OXFORD MELBOURNE AUCKLAND
JOHANNESBURG BLANTYRE GABORONE
IBADAN PORTSMOUTH (NH) USA CHICAGO

05 04 03 02 01
10 9 8 7 6 5 4 3 2 1

ISBN 0 431 14301 3 (HB)
ISBN 0 431 14307 2 (PB)

British Library Cataloguing in Publication Data

Parker, Steve, 1952 -
Plastic. - (Science files)
1. Plastics
I. Title
620.1'923

Printed and bound in Spain by Bookprint, S.L., Barcelona

PHOTO CREDITS :
Abbreviations: t-top, m-middle, b-bottom, r-right,
l-left.

Front cover - br & 4/5 (François Souse), bl & 18/19
(Pascal Goetgheluck) - Science Photo Library. tr, 3 &
10/11 - Spectrum Colour Library. 5br & 28tr (P. Van
Riel), 9tl (Nigel Francis), 18bl (Avend/Smith), 19tr
(Mark Mawson), 23tr - Robert Harding Picture
Library. 12bl, 15tl (Deep Light Productions), 12tr
(Klaus Guldbrandsen), 14 (Geoff Tompkinson), 15m
(Maximilian Stock Ltd), 16bl (NASA), 25bl, 29bl
(Adam Hart-Davis), 28bl (Ron Sanford) - Science
Photo Library. 26bl (Eric Horan), 24bl, 26/27t, 29tl -
Spectrum Colour Library. 6m, 6br, 13tr - Ann Ronan
Picture Library. 9br, 11br, 20/21b - British Plastics
Foundation. 23br (Kev Robertson), 27bl (Robert
Cianflone) - Allsport. 22/23b - Hulton Getty.

Every effort has been made to trace the copyright
holders and we apologise in advance for any
unintentional omissions. We would be pleased to
insert the appropriate acknowledgement in any
subsequent edition of this publication.

*An explanation of difficult words can be
found in the glossary on page 30.*

SCIENCE FILES

PLASTICS

Steve Parker

Heinemann LIBRARY

CONTENTS

Disposable gloves, food cartons, bath sponges, soccer balls – they are all made from different types of plastics.

INTRODUCTION

Do you use a TV, a writing pen or a computer? Have you been in a car, bus, train or plane? Wherever you are, so are plastics. These substances are vital in today's world. Not only are they useful and important in everyday life. Plastics are also essential in machines, industries and factories. But they can bring trouble. Some plastics cause waste problems and pollution. And because of the way they are made, we cannot keep producing new plastics for ever. Recycling and re-use are important for all our resources, but especially for plastics.

New plastics are invented for space suits, spacecraft, rockets and satellites. Some find extra uses down here on Earth.

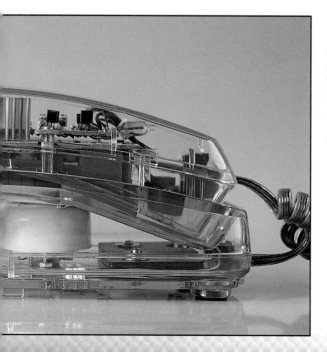

This telephone has a see-through plastic case. It keeps the insides clean and safe, yet still on view.

Years ago, plastics were simply thrown away. Now many kinds are made so that they can be easily collected and recycled.

Some of the substances we use every day come direct from nature, like wood. But plastics do not. They have to be made, or manufactured, from raw materials. These raw materials include crude oil, coal, natural gas, minerals and plants.

Most crude oil (petroleum) is found deep underground. It comes up through holes drilled from tall towers, or derricks.

RAW MATERIALS

The first plastic-type materials were made more than 100 years ago, from cellulose. This natural substance is found in plant materials such as cotton and wood. Cellulose was heated with chemicals such as acids and camphor. The result was a strange new, hard, shiny material that did not go dull or rot away. Chemist Alexander Parkes (1813–90) produced this type of plastic in about 1858. It became known as celluloid.

The first cars to be mass-produced were Model T Fords, from about 1913. As the need for petrol rose, the oil industry became a huge business.

Oil wells, 1866.

Crude oil is a mixture of hundreds of substances. It is heated in huge, tall towers called fractionation columns. This separates the oil into different parts, or fractions. The gases and lighter liquids come from the top of the tower, where conditions are hottest. Some of the other fractions from oil are used to make plastics.

Petroleum gases and vapours

Fractionation tower

Petrols (gasolines)

Jet fuels (kerosenes) and paraffin

Diesel oils

Light lubricating and fuel oils

Crude oil

Steam

Heavy, thick fuel and lubricating oils

Waxes, asphalts and bitumens

Crude oil is taken by pipelines or supertanker ships to giant oil refineries. Here the oil is separated into many different and useful substances.

Facts from the **PAST**

At first, crude oil was mainly burned in lamps. The first oil wells were drilled in about 1859 in Titusville, Pennsylvania, USA. But people gradually discovered many other useful substances in oil. One was petrol for the first cars. From the 1920s onwards, others were used to make plastics.

LEFTOVER OIL

From the 1900s, cars became popular. Their fuel was petrol, which came from oil (petroleum). But taking petrol out of oil left various unwanted substances. What could be done with them? Chemists gradually discovered: make them into plastics!

CHEMISTRY OF PLASTICS

All substances, including plastics, are made of tiny parts called atoms and molecules. There are only a few types of atoms in most plastics. The main ones are carbon (C) and hydrogen (H). These join to make simple molecules called hydrocarbons.

Facts from the **PAST**
The second main type of plastic was invented in 1907 by Leo Baekeland. He made it by heating together two chemicals, formaldehyde and phenol. Named Bakelite, it did not carry or conduct electricity. So it made safe casings for electrical items.

The plastic called polyethylene is made of thousands of small molecules, known as ethylenes, joined together in long rows. 'Poly-' in this sense means 'many'.

Links (bonds) between atoms

Hydrogen atom

ETHYLENE MOLECULES

Carbon atom

POLYETHYLENE (PLASTIC)

LINKED TOGETHER

Most hydrocarbon molecules are naturally small. Ethylene has only two carbon atoms and four hydrogen ones (C_2H_4). The key to making plastics is to join hundreds or thousands of these small molecules together into long chains.

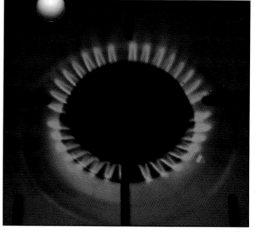

Bottled gases such as propane and butane, which we burn in cookers, stoves and lamps, are hydrocarbons – similar to the monomers of plastics.

Bakelite telephone (1930s).

MONOMERS AND POLYMERS

The small molecules, like ethylene, are called monomers. The giant ones, formed by linking thousands of monomers into long rows, are called polymers. This is why the names of so many plastics begin with 'poly', such as polystyrene, and polyvinyl chloride (PVC).

MAKING PLASTICS

Most raw materials for plastics come from crude oil, split into its different parts and treated with various chemicals. The raw materials are heated to exactly the right temperature.

Often pigments (colouring substances) are added. In this example, styrene monomers join into polymers – the plastic polystyrene. It is light and brittle, and often used as 'foam plastic'.

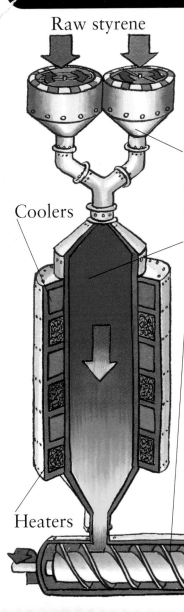

Raw styrene

Coolers

Heaters

Cutter

1 Styrene monomers begin to join together in stir tanks, with the aid of other chemicals

2 Small polymers link into longer ones in a carefully heated reactor vessel

3 The hot, liquid plastic is forced along a tube by a screw-shaped extruder

4 Plastic cools and hardens in a water tank and is cut into chips

9

Coloured plastic chips and granules.

There are hundreds of different kinds of plastics, and new types are invented every year. But most plastics can be put into one of two main groups, depending on what happens when they are heated. These two groups are called the thermoplastics and the thermosets. ('Thermo' means 'heat'.)

TO MELT OR NOT TO MELT?

The main way of shaping plastics, as shown on later pages, is to heat them until they become melted and runny, or molten. The molten plastic is poured into shapes called moulds. It cools and goes hard, ready for use. If a thermoplastic is heated again, it melts. But a thermoset stays hard and keeps its shape.

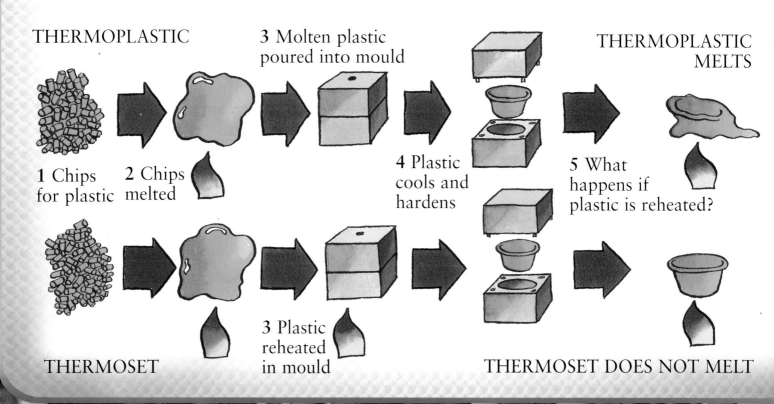

THERMOPLASTIC

1 Chips for plastic   2 Chips melted

3 Molten plastic poured into mould

4 Plastic cools and hardens

5 What happens if plastic is reheated?

THERMOPLASTIC MELTS

THERMOSET

3 Plastic reheated in mould

THERMOSET DOES NOT MELT

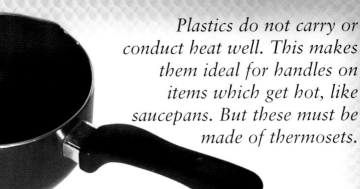

Plastics do not carry or conduct heat well. This makes them ideal for handles on items which get hot, like saucepans. But these must be made of thermosets.

IMPORTANCE OF HEAT

The difference between thermoplastics and thermosets makes them suitable for different uses. Plastics which are exposed to heat must be thermosets. Thermoplastics can be melted down and re-used or recycled more easily.

Each type of plastic is specialized for certain uses. Many toys are made of plastic which is tough but soft, without sharp edges.

Ideas for the FUTURE

Most plastic parts and items are mass-produced in factories. But one day, the Instant Plastics Shop may sell all kinds and colours of plastic. These could be shaped by a computer within seconds, to form any object you can imagine.

Any design in an instant?

PROPERTIES OF PLASTICS

Although there are hundreds of kinds of plastics, most have similar properties or features. They are lightweight and fairly tough. They do not rot away and they are little affected by rain, ice and bad weather. They resist carrying heat and electricity. Many can be made with smooth, shiny surfaces and bright colours. Some plastics are flexible and bend easily; others are stiff and brittle, and if they are bent, they snap.

11

Toy building bricks must all be precisely the same size and shape. Otherwise they would not fit tightly together.

Most plastic objects are made from chips, granules or powders of plastic, produced by heating the raw materials or ingredients. The chips are put into bags or tanks and stored, and taken to the moulding machines.

MAKING PLASTIC WITH MOULDS

The plastic chips or granules are heated until they become soft, or even molten (melted and runny). They are poured or pushed into a hollow metal shape, the mould. The soft, flexible plastic takes on this shape, then cools hard. The mould is taken apart to release the plastic object.

Before plastic powder is poured into a moulding machine, workers check that it is the right colour and type of plastic.

MOULDING METHODS 1

INJECTION MOULDING

The plastic chips from a hopper are fed into a screw-like device. This pushes them at great pressure past heaters. The high temperature and pressure makes the plastic go soft. It is forced or injected into the mould, where it sets – goes solid and hard.

1 Plastic chips

3 Heaters

2 Screw-injector

4 Mould

5 Product

EXACT COPIES

Using a mould to make plastic items means that every item is the same shape and size. Each type of moulding has its special uses. For example, rotational moulding (shown below) makes circular or rounded objects which are hollow. These include balls, litter bins, storage drums, lamp shades, cylinders and tanks. (More moulding methods are shown on the next page.)

(More moulding methods are shown on the next page.)

Facts from the **PAST**

Mass-production of plastic objects such as toys meant that they could be made quickly and cheaply. From the 1950s, this led to a huge boom in sales. Before this, every toy had to be shaped by hand, from materials such as wood.

Assembling parts into toy dolls.

The mould or form gives its shape, including any patterns, exactly to the plastic object.

ROTATIONAL MOULDING

Soft, runny plastic is put into the mould, then the mould spins or rotates at high speed while still hot. This spreads the plastic as a thin, even layer around the inside of the mould. The plastic is cooled by jets of cold air or water spray while the mould still spins.

1 Liquid plastic put into mould

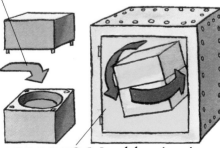

2 Mould spins in oven   **3** Product

DIP MOULDING

This method uses a cast or form, where plastic is put on the outside, rather than a mould, where it is on the inside. The cast dips in a bath of hot, runny plastic. It comes out coated with a thin layer, which stays flexible even when cool.

2 Cast dips in

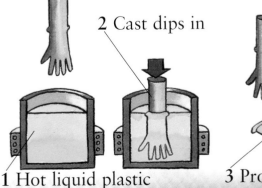

1 Hot liquid plastic   **3** Product

Factory machines produce thousands of items every minute. Quality control workers check them regularly to make sure there are no faults.

There are various ways of moulding plastics into the shapes of the finished items. Some ways are shown here and on the previous pages. These methods make plastics different from many other materials.

LESS WASTE AND COST

Objects made from wood or stone are usually shaped by cutting, carving and sanding. Gradually the unwanted material is removed from a large block, to leave the shape of the item. Plastic objects are already shaped when made, cutting down on waste, time and cost.

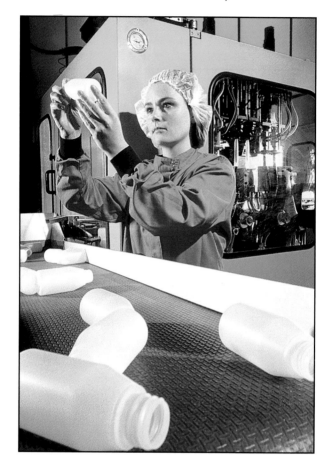

MOULDING METHODS 2

EXTRUSION MOULDING

Plastic pellets are squeezed at high pressure and heated. They are forced past a metal shape, the form or die, to make the product.

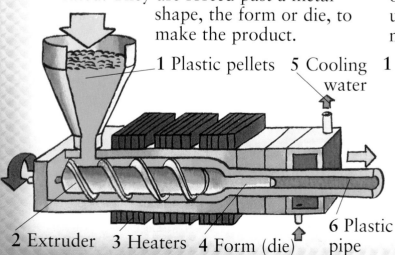

1 Plastic pellets
5 Cooling water
2 Extruder 3 Heaters 4 Form (die) 6 Plastic pipe

BLOW MOULDING

A blob of runny plastic is put on to the end of a tube. Air or gas at high pressure blows it up like a balloon, pressing it against the mould to make a hollow shape.

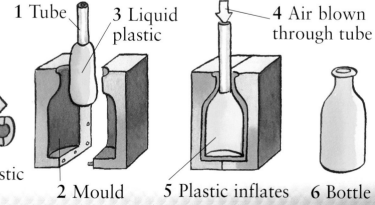

1 Tube 3 Liquid plastic 4 Air blown through tube
2 Mould 5 Plastic inflates 6 Bottle

Making the moulds that shape plastics is a skilled task. Several versions may be produced to obtain the exact shape.

Ideas for the FUTURE

One of the main features of plastics is that they are hardly attacked by moulds and fungus. So they do not rot away. But in the future, could a new bug appear that attacked plastic materials? Then all plastic items might rot and decay before our eyes!

Will plastics have to be germ-free?

LONG AND THIN

Different types of plastics are suited to different ways of moulding, to make different products. The plastic called polypropylene is tough but also flexible. It can be drawn out into very long, thin shapes, like pipes and tubes, by extrusion moulding.

VACUUM MOULDING

A thin, heated, softened sheet of plastic is put over the mould. A vacuum pump removes air from between the sheet and mould. The sheet sucks down tightly and takes on the mould's shape.

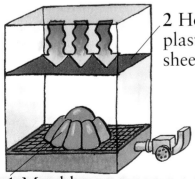

2 Hot plastic sheet

1 Mould

3 Vacuum pump

4 Plastic sucks down and presses over mould

5 Product

Vacuum moulding or 'vac-forming' is used for tray-like shapes such as blister packs and toy cartons.

Some plastic objects have hardly any plastic in them at all. They are mostly air (or some kind of gas). They are as lightweight as feathers, and are known as foam or foamed plastics.

LOTS OF BUBBLES

In a foamed plastic, there are many spaces or bubbles surrounded by lightweight plastic. Sometimes the bubbles are big enough to see. In other cases they are microscopic.

Ideas for the **FUTURE**

Plastics should never be eaten. They are not nutritious, and the body cannot digest them. But far in the future, special foamed plastics could be made with nutrients, proteins, vitamins and flavours. They would make a tasty, healthy 'light snack'!

Plastic foods – a taste in space?

MANY USES

Foamed or spongy plastics have hundreds of uses. Some make packaging, like cartons and cases for foods, toys, electronic gadgets and delicate items. Others are made into plastic 'worms' that fill the gaps around large, heavy items in big crates and boxes. These foamed plastics are generally soft and help to cushion the item against knocks and bumps. They are also very light, so they add hardly any weight to the whole package.

Stiff foam plastics make waterproof, strong, rigid cartons for foods and toys. Softer, flexible types of foamed plastics soak up water into their holes and are used for sponges.

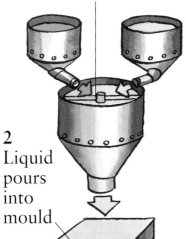

1 Chemicals mixed

2 Liquid pours into mould

3 Bubbles expand and plastic sets hard

Plastics are made into bubble-filled foams in two main ways.

◄Foamed polyurethane is made by mixing two chemicals, isocyanate and polyol, with acids and a foaming chemical. The mixture sets hard and rigid in a mould.

►Foamed polystyrene (Styrofoam) is made in the form of beads with a blowing chemical added. The beads are melted and moulded when the blowing agent gives off gases that form the bubbles.

1 Polystyrene beads containing blowing chemical

2 Beads are heated and poured into mould

3 More heating makes blowing chemical form bubbles

KEEPING WARM

Heat does not pass easily through most plastics, nor through bubbles of air. This means foamed plastics are very useful as insulation. Large sheets or smaller chips are put behind walls, floors and ceilings, to keep the heat in. Or, in the case of cold-store rooms, to keep the heat out!

Large sheets of foamed or expanded polystyrene are used to slow down the passage of heat (or cold) and sound.

In almost any street, anywhere in the world, there are plastic carrier bags. They hold foods, drinks, clothes, shopping and anything else you can imagine.

THIN AND FLEXIBLE

Polyethylene (polythene, see page 8) is very adaptable. It can be made in many hardnesses and thicknesses, depending on which chemicals are added to it. No other plastic is manufactured in such huge amounts. One of its main products is very thin, paper-like sheets or films, like those used to make carrier bags.

Flexible plastics can be shaped into umbrellas, raincoats and similar water-proof items.

In the plastic bag factory, a tube of thin plastic is blown up and cooled by powerful blasts of air.

Facts from the PAST

In the 1880s one of the first plastics, celluloid (see page 6), was made more flexible by adding different chemicals. The new bendy version, cellulose nitrate, was produced as long, thin strips of sheets or films. Other chemicals on it recorded photographs. These became the first movies – 'films'.

Films on plastic films.

USED EVERYWHERE

Light, strong, bendy, weather-resistant and waterproof – thin plastic sheets and films have endless uses. Sweet wrappers, clingfilm for food, shower curtains, play-tents, umbrellas, black dustbin-bags and all-weather clothing are just a few. (See also page 24.)

BLOWING BAGS

The plastic used for films and sheets is usually low-density polyethylene. It is not heavy, or dense, but light and flexible, yet still strong. Its polymer molecules point in many different directions, like a handful of drinking straws dropped on the ground. High-density polyethylene is much heavier and stiffer. Its polymer molecules are lined up in bundles.

1 Plastic pellets

6 Thin-walled tube

5 Blast of air inflates tube

4 Melted plastic

7 Rollers flatten tube for sealing

8 Sealer

2 Extruder

3 Heaters

9 Slicer

10 Plastic bags

19

Some plastic looks exactly like glass. It's hard and tough, and perfectly clear, so you can see through it. It looks just like window glass – but it's plastic.

Vehicle windscreens are made from layers of clear plastic and toughened glass, called laminates.

PLASTIC GLASS

One of the main plastics used to make clear sheets is acrylic. Its chemical name is polymethyl methacrylate (PMMA). It's also known as Perspex, Plexiglass or Lucite. It does not shatter into sharp pieces like glass. It just cracks, and so it is safer.

Hard, clear plastics are moulded smooth or with shapes like lines and numbers (left).

MANY USES

Clear acrylic and polycarbonate are used for roofs and windows. They can be moulded into complex shapes such as curved vehicle lights. Being impact-resistant or shatterproof, they make windscreens on motorcycles, speedboats and helicopters, and protective equipment such as cycle helmets.

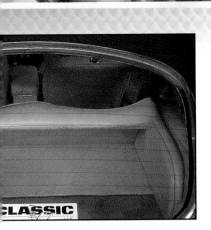

TEXTURED PLASTICS

Many plastic objects are made with surfaces that are smooth and shiny, to look good and resist wear. But some plastic sheets need a surface which is slightly uneven, with textures such as grooves or wrinkles.

The surface texture is pressed into the hot, soft plastic as it is made into a sheet. The pressing is done by a roller which has the same surface pattern, but in reverse. This pressing method is called embossing.

1 Plastic pellets

2 Heated roller melts plastic

3 Embossing roller presses pattern into surface

4 Embossed plastic sheet

Embossed plastics can be coloured and patterned so they look and feel like natural materials, such as leather, cloth or wood.

Flexible sheets of heated plastic such as PVC (polyvinyl chloride) are pressed by a series of rollers on a machine. This is known as calendering.

21

RUBBERY PLASTICS

Natural rubber is fairly soft and bendy, and bounces back when squeezed or stretched. It comes from plants such as rubber trees, and is usually very expensive. But some plastics can be made to look and feel almost exactly like rubber. They include PVC and ABS (see below).

MIXING PLASTICS

Some plastic materials contain more than one type of monomer (basic chemical). They are a combination of several monomers. These types of plastics are known as co-polymers.

ABS contains three types of monomers – acrylonitrile, butadiene and styrene. By mixing these in different amounts, ABS can be made hard and stiff, or soft and rubbery.

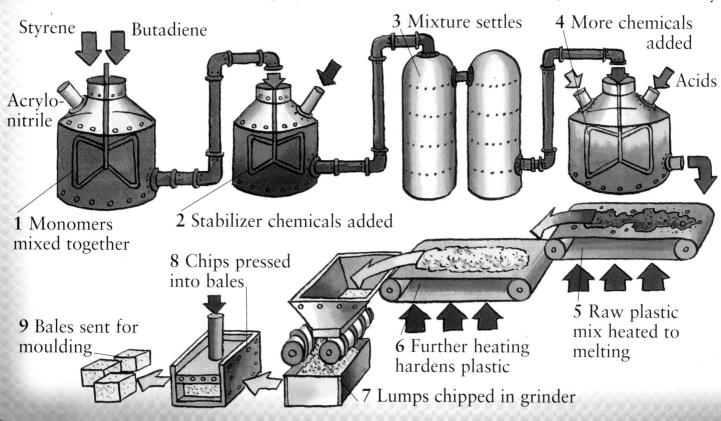

Styrene Butadiene

Acrylo-nitrile

3 Mixture settles

4 More chemicals added

Acids

1 Monomers mixed together

2 Stabilizer chemicals added

8 Chips pressed into bales

9 Bales sent for moulding

5 Raw plastic mix heated to melting

6 Further heating hardens plastic

7 Lumps chipped in grinder

Vehicle tyres are usually a mixture of natural rubber and the tough, hard-wearing, flexible plastic called SBR, styrene-butadiene rubber.

A diving suit bends with the body's movements. It is also slightly foamed for protection and to keep the diver warm.

'COOKING' WITH PLASTICS

Making plastics is sometimes like cooking! The end result depends on which ingredients are used. The plastic polybutadiene is bendy and squishy, like rubber, but too soft to make items such as vehicle tyres. The plastic polystyrene is much harder and more brittle. Add the two together in the correct amounts, and the result is bendy, squishy and tough.

ARTIFICIAL RUBBERS

Plastics with features of natural rubber, such as springing back when squashed, are called synthetic or artificial rubbers. They are used for flexible, waterproof items such as bendy tubing, seals, connectors and torches. Foamed versions make soft, padded 'foam rubber' cushions for furniture.

Rubbery plastics make clothes which are bendy, stretchy and waterproof.

Facts from the PAST

Natural rubber, like plastic, is a polymer. It contains long chains of the monomer called isoprene, and so it is known as polyisoprene. The first plastic-based artificial rubbers, such as SBR (see above), were made in the USA in the 1940s.

Tyres use up two-thirds of all rubber, natural and artificial.

Some items made of plastic, such as buckets or carrier bags, contain almost nothing except the plastic. However, plastics are also added to other substances, to make a huge variety of different materials with thousands of uses.

ADDING PLASTIC

Plastics can be moulded into sheets, for items such as clothes, covers and boat sails. However, once a sheet of plastic is slightly broken at the edge, it tears very easily. Another method is to weave the items out of fibres like cotton, to make cloth in the usual way – then add the plastic. This can give the benefits of both materials.

PLASTICS AND FABRICS

Plastic gives extra waterproofing.

Plastics can be combined with cloths, or fabrics, in various ways. For plastic-impregnated cloth, the fabric passes through warm plastic paste. Then heaters make the plastic run between, or impregnate, the fibres of the cloth. Or a sheet of plastic is 'ironed' on to the cloth, so that it melts slightly and sticks to the fibres. The result is a plastic surface one side and cloth on the other.

5 Plastic-impregnated cloth product

4 Drier-coolers

1 Roll of cloth

3 Heaters melt plastic into fabric

2 Cloth passes through tank of plastic paste

PLASTIC PLUS PAINTS

Plastics are very important in all kinds of paints. They help the paint to brush on smoothly. They make the paint's pigments (coloured substances) spread evenly so the colours are not blotchy. They give bulk or thickness to the layer of paint, and help it to stick to the surface beneath. And they form a hard-wearing, shiny surface when the paint is dry. Some types of paints, like the acrylics used by artists, are named after the type of plastics in them.

Plastics, fillers, pigments, smoothers, solvents and many other substances are mixed together for special-purpose paints.

Plastic resins help to stick together, or bind, the tiny particles of pigments and other substances, to make smooth-spreading paint.

Tiny grains of clear plastic catch the light and throw it back out again. This process, reflection, helps bright colours to shine in the dimness.

Ideas for the **FUTURE**

Some plastics seem to change colour, depending on how the light shines on them. A future plastic might really change colour when certain kinds of rays shine on to it, from a ray-gun. Paint it on to the walls, and you could change a room's colour in a few seconds!

Which colour today?

25

Plastics are familiar from everyday items such as bags and buckets. They are also used in the latest high-technology machines and equipment, such as space rockets, racing cars, stealth planes and jet engines. In fact, research to find better plastics helps to bring new and improved versions into daily life. One example is the non-stick frying pan!

Plastics added to artificial fibres make materials strong enough to cover huge areas, without sagging or tearing.

Plastics combined with Kevlar, an artificial-fibre fabric, make a rip-proof material. Its uses include sails, hang-glider wings and bullet-proof clothing.

Space suits and jet packs contain at least 25 kinds of specialized, very lightweight plastics.

NON-STICK, LOTS OF SLIP

The plastic with the very long chemical name of polytetrafluoroethylene is also known as PTFE or Teflon. It's very hard and tough, and resists heat, chemicals and electricity. It is also very slippery, and used for non-stick surfaces.

Teflon does not become soft until heated above 320°C. It coats non-stick pans and is also used in high-temperature machines and tools.

COMPOSITES

Plastics can be mixed with other substances, such as carbon-fibres, metals or glass-fibres, to make materials called composites. The substances in a composite are altered for its special job, including hi-tech sports equipment – from tennis racquets to Olympic racing bicycles.

Facts from the PAST

In the 1960s, scientists invented the Futuro – a lightweight, portable house made from plastics. A small crane could move it from place to place. The chairs, tables and beds were all part of the moulded design. So were the heaters, water pipes and electrical systems. From the outside, the Futuro looked like a 'flying saucer'!

In the Futuro plastic house.

Carbon-fibre composites make light, tough parts for fast motorbikes, bicycles, cars, boats and planes. The mix of plastic and fibre is strong yet slightly flexible.

Plastics are an essential part of today's world, with thousands of uses. But they also bring various problems. Two of these problems are the raw materials we use to make plastics, and how we get rid of plastics.

THE OIL CRISIS

Most plastics are made from crude oil (petroleum). About one-twentieth of oil is used for this purpose. The rest goes to make fuels and other substances. But we are using oil so fast, Earth's supplies may run out within 100 years. If they do, so will most plastics.

It's best to collect the different types of plastics separately, for recycling. This saves time and money sorting them later.

Plastic-based ropes, nets, string, bottles and crates stay around for years. As well as polluting the environment, they are dangers to wildlife.

Ideas for the **FUTURE**

A few kinds of plastics are made to biodegrade, or rot away naturally. Years from now, perhaps we could alter the genes of animals such as spiders or silkworms, so they spin plastic-type fibres. We would collect these strong fibres and put them to all kinds of uses, like spider-silk clothes! Eventually the fibres would biodegrade for recycling by nature.

Recycling plastics is complicated. Different types must be processed in different ways. Some can be melted or ground up, and used to make more plastic products such as bottles, bags, cartons, crates, fences, posts, garden seats, sheets, bricks, tiles and pipes. Others are spun into fluffy, fleecy fibres. Some can be burned as fuel to power their own recycling.

Plastics make up about one-tenth of the weight of waste thrown away by people in rich countries.

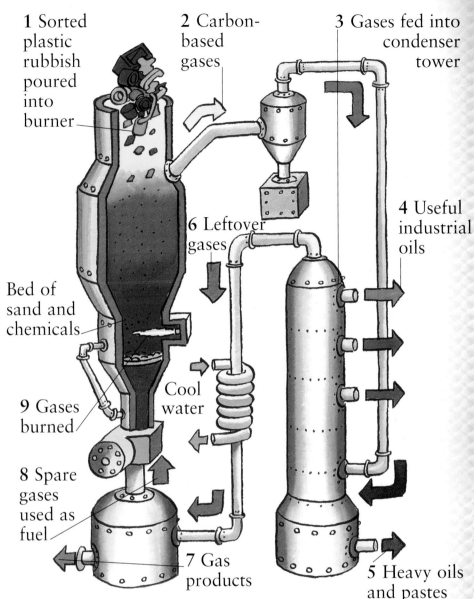

1 Sorted plastic rubbish poured into burner

2 Carbon-based gases

3 Gases fed into condenser tower

4 Useful industrial oils

6 Leftover gases

Bed of sand and chemicals

Cool water

9 Gases burned

8 Spare gases used as fuel

7 Gas products

5 Heavy oils and pastes

Spider 'farms' for plastics?

NOT NATURAL

Natural substances such as wood and leather biodegrade, which means they rot away or decay, back into the soil. Most plastics are not natural, so they do not biodegrade. They will last for hundreds, even thousands, of years. For these two reasons, production and disposal, it is very important to conserve, save, recycle and reuse all kinds of plastics.

NOTE Many plastics have several names, including the name of the main monomer, the name of the polymer, brand names, trade names, manufacturers' names and inventor's name.

TYPE OF PLASTIC		FEATURES AND USES
THERMOPLASTICS	Acrylonitrile-buta-diene-styrene (ABS)	Resists impact, used for pipes, tubes, car parts, casings, tools, small appliances, fridge door linings, protective equipment
	Acrylic (PMMA)	Transparent, hard, strong, used for safety 'glass', signs, reflectors, light cases, fibres in textiles
	Celluloid	Flexible when thin, shiny, tended to burst into flames, was used for decorative objects, movie films
	Polycarbonate	Clear, strong, used for windows, safety 'glass', traffic signs, household and office equipment
	Polyethylene (polythene)	Adaptable, flexible, durable, low-density used for films, bags, bottles, high-density for pipes, crates, pressure equipment
	Polytetrafluoro-ethylene (PTFE, Teflon)	Very resistant to chemicals, electricity and heat (even though thermoplastic), low friction (very slippery), used for heat-resistant and non-stick coatings and surfaces, insulation
	Polypropylene	Tough, flexible, extrudes well, used for pipes, tubes, household equipment, crates, medical items such as artificial joints
	Polystyrene	Fairly brittle but readily made into foamed or expanded versions, used for packaging, toys, floating items like lifesavers
	Polyvinyl chloride (PVC) or 'vinyl'	Strong, adaptable, resists sunlight and weather, used for artificial leather, clothes, window frames, tiles and flooring
THERMOSETS	Epoxy-resin plastics	Hard, resist chemicals, heat, electricity, impacts, used for electrical equipment, flooring, sports gear, structural panels
	Phenol-formaldehyde (Bakelite, melamine)	Resists heat, chemicals and electricity, hard and strong, used for pan handles, knobs, electrical equipment such as plugs and sockets, laminates, plastic plates and tableware
	Polyurethane	Foams well, used for furniture, padding, insulation, sports equipment, packaging

GLOSSARY

biodegrade
To rot away, decay or break down naturally into simpler substances such as minerals, by the action of microbes, moulds and other living things.

composite
A material made by combining very different types of substances, such as plastic, metal and fibres.

co-polymer
A very large chemical grouping or molecule, made from two or more kinds of smaller units (monomers) joined together.

extrusion
When a substance is pulled or drawn out into a long, thin shape, such as a tube, rod, pipe or wire.

foam
A liquid or solid containing lots of spaces or bubbles. Soap foam in the bathtub is a liquid-based foam. A sponge or foamed plastic is a solid-based foam.

impact-resistant
Being able to stand up to hard knocks and bumps without breaking, or at least without shattering into pieces.

insulation
Resisting or preventing the flow of electricity (electrical insulation) or heat (thermal insulation).

molten
Melted, as a runny or syrupy liquid.

monomer
One of the small chemical units, or molecules, which joins to many copies of itself, like links in a chain, to make a polymer.

petroleum
Crude oil – the thick, dark, gooey substance found in the ground. Often simply called 'oil'.

polymer
A very large chemical grouping or molecule, made from many smaller units (monomers) joined together.